God's Word
and Your Life

Think

Ask

Bible

God's Word and Your Life

What the Bible Says about Social Media, Money and other Exciting Stuff!

Laura Martin

CF4·K

Copyright © Laura Martin 2016

10 9 8 7 6 5 4 3 2 1

Paperback ISBN: 978-1-78191-822-7

e-pub ISBN: 978-1-78191-923-3

mobi ISBN: 978-1-78191-930-9

First published in 2016 by

Christian Focus Publications Ltd,

Geanies House, Fearn, Ross-shire

IV20 1TW, Scotland

www.christianfocus.com

Cover and internal page design by Pete Barnsley (Creativehoot.com)

Printed and bound by Bell and Bain, Glasgow

MIX
Paper from
responsible sources
FSC® C007785
www.fsc.org

FROM THE AUTHOR TO YOU

My name is Laura Martin and I'm married to Bryan. We have five beautiful children and a crazy spaniel. I serve alongside my husband, who is pastor of River City Bible Church – a church we planted in Hamilton, New Zealand in 2010. Prior to that we were serving in a church in the U.K. I home-school our children, enjoy travelling, gardening, quilting, projects around the house, and writing. I love to disciple and counsel from God's precious Word. Thank you for reading!

Laura Martin

You can contact Laura at: laureemartin75@gmail.com

Dedication

For the young people at River City Bible Church.
We are so blessed to have you as a part of our church family.
Keep your eyes on Jesus!
Mrs M

'And it is my prayer that your love may abound more and more, with knowledge and all discernment, so that you may approve what is excellent and so be pure and blameless for the day of Christ, filled with the fruit of righteousness that comes through Jesus Christ, to the glory and praise of God.'
—Philippians 1:9-11

Contents

What does the Bible say about...?

What does the
Bible Say about...

Social Media?

Think

Ask

Bible

There were once two women who were living, for a time at least, in the same house. Both of them had a baby within three days of each other, and very sadly one of the babies died during the night. An argument arose between the two women over who the living baby belonged to. One woman argued the live baby was hers. The other woman argued that it was hers. 'Your baby died! You took my baby and swapped him for yours!' one cried. 'No! This is my baby. Your baby was the one that died!' No one else was in the house with them at the time so there was no witness to help them sort out this terrible and tragic argument. What should they do? They did the only thing they could do, they went to King Solomon, the wisest king in all of history.

> Then the king said, 'One says, "This is my son that is alive, and your son is dead'; and the other says, 'No; but your son is dead, and my son is the living one.'" And the king said, 'Bring me a sword.' So a sword was brought before the king. And the king said, 'Divide the living child in two, and give half to one and half to the other.' Then the woman whose son was alive said to the king, because her heart yearned for her son, 'Oh, my lord, give her the living child, and by no means put him to death.' But the other said, 'He shall be neither mine nor yours; divide him.' Then the king answered and said, 'Give the living child to the first woman, and by no means put him to death; she is his mother.'
>
> —1 Kings 3:23-27

Remember when God had appeared to Solomon and promised to give him whatever he asked for? Solomon asked for wisdom. He was wise enough to know that he was not wise enough to be king of Israel. He needed God's wisdom, and that is exactly what we see in action here: God's wisdom. Could Solomon have gone to the Holy Scriptures and found an answer to the problem of women fighting over a baby? No. But Scripture contains principles from which we can make decisions or answer questions. How does that happen?

Let's look at a biblical principle Solomon would have known in this situation (remembering that although he did not have the Bible as we do, God gave Solomon the same wisdom that we have in our Bibles).

For where your treasure is, there your heart will be also.

—Matthew 6:21

Solomon knew that the woman who treasured this baby could not allow him to be harmed. That proved correct. As soon as he suggested dividing the baby in two so that both woman could have him, the true mother cried out in motherly distress. She could not allow her precious baby to be killed – even if it meant that she would not have him.

When the people in the city heard how Solomon dealt with these two women, they were amazed. No doubt they wondered, 'How did he know to suggest such a terrible thing? How did he know the real mother would never allow her baby to be killed?' But we know, don't we? God gave Solomon wisdom. And now God has given us wisdom, in the form of wise principles from His Word the Bible that we can apply to life's situations. Just as Solomon did that day.

Now, that perhaps seems a strange way to start a chapter on what the Bible teaches about social media. But actually there is a similarity between the case of the dead and living babies, and social media. Can you think what that similarity might be?

The answer is, the Bible does not speak about a 'baby-war' or about social media. But just as God gave Solomon wisdom as to how to deal with the fighting mothers, He has also given us wisdom as to how to think about social media.

So … let's start off with a simple question. What exactly is social media? Very basically, social media is an online 'place' that enables you to communicate with others.

Now, I don't know what rules you might have in your home about going online, but that's okay. At some point you will no doubt be online in some way, so this is just as useful for you as it is for your neighbour who maybe already has a Facebook account.

Perhaps (hopefully) your parents and your teachers have spent some time with you talking through the dangers of being online, being 'friended' by people you don't know, the bullying that can happen and the ways in which you can protect your privacy. If not, it might be a good thing for you to ask to have some time to discuss that together. So, I won't go into any of that now. Instead, we are going to take a slightly different approach.

Did You Know ...?

According to Google, about 4 million blog posts are read everyday. That's one post for every person in New Zealand every day!

Facebook has said that there are over one billion regular Facebook users. That is about the same number as the population of the continent of Africa. Wow! And what is Facebook? It's just a place where you can share whatever you like, including photos of what you did today and what you had for dinner! You are free to write whatever is on your mind, and post it. Boom! As soon as you push 'post', everyone who is allowed access to your account suddenly has your words and photos on their 'news feed' (a page which shows all their friends' posts). It is a wonderful way to keep in touch with people who don't live local to you (and even those who do). But it has its pitfalls too.

Blogging is another way to keep in touch. Some people use a blog as a diary – perhaps your class at school does this. It allows parents to see some of what you are up to each day. It can be a lot of fun. But just as with Facebook, as soon as you push 'post', your words and images are 'out there' for the world to see.

So if social media is so fun, why do we need principles from the Bible to help us to think about how we use it? Well, let's see....

Let's look at the 'treasure principle' that we spoke of earlier in the chapter and see how it applies to social media.

For where your treasure is, there your heart will be also.
—Matthew 6:21

You might be wondering if it does in fact apply to social media. But trust me, it does. One of the things about social media is that it is a two-way communication. Whether you are on Facebook or on a blog, or some other online 'place', when you post something, others have the opportunity to respond by writing something back or by 'liking' it. This is where a problem might arise. When someone writes a nice comment back, or pushes 'like', it feels pretty good. Sometimes it might even feel great. So then we might be tempted to write or post other things that will get more 'nice' responses from people. We can become like those who treasure the approval of others more than anything else. So we try to anticipate what people will like to see from us, instead of just being ourselves. We find our treasure in 'being liked' by others and for some people it becomes a serious thing that they can't live without. And the opposite is true also. If someone makes an unkind comment back, it can be very hurtful and cause you to want to respond in anger and/or write things that make people say nice things to make you feel better.

What about 'selfies'? Many find their treasure in how they look. Often the first place a selfie picture goes is online. Recently, our family went for a big walk up to the top of a mountain. It's not a huge walk and there are a lot of people who do it each day for fitness, but it's worth doing just for the views; they are breath taking. So we reached the top of the mountain where there is a large grassy area. My husband, our five children and I all sat down and got out the water bottles. We were just quietly enjoying the view when I realised that we were the only ones not taking selfies. And straight away, many of them were posted online. I can imagine the comments that came back: 'Wow, you are amazing, I could never have done that!' or 'Wow, you're looking awesome!', or 'Wow, I wish I was there.' All comments that make the 'model' feel great and popular and lucky! We need to be careful .... Where our treasure is, there our heart will be also. Make sure your heart is not looking for the approval of others rather than the approval of God.

Keep your heart with all vigilance, for from it flows the springs of life.
—Proverbs 4:23

But how do we do that?

Jesus said to him, 'I am the way, the truth and the life. No one comes to the Father except through me.'
—John 14:6

What does vigilance mean? It means to keep a watch out for danger. So this verse from Proverbs is telling us to keep a watch out for things that are a danger to our hearts (minds). Why? Because from it flow springs of life.

We need to make Jesus our treasure because He is life. How do we make Jesus our treasure? By believing in Him as our Saviour, turning from our sin and following Him all the days of our lives. Only then will life flow from our hearts. Be sure to treasure the right thing (Jesus), and then be on guard against things that might cause you to make something else your treasure in Jesus' place.

But wait, there's more!

What other Principles can we Learn from Scripture?

Bible

There are so many principles that we could apply to how we use and think about social media. I'll share just a few more.

1. Watch your words

> *Let your speech always be gracious, seasoned with salt, so that you may know how you ought to answer each person.*
>
> —Colossians 4:6

It's interesting that salt should be used to season our speech, isn't it? But salt has some very handy uses. It can preserve food to keep it from rotting. It can make food tastier by bringing out flavour. It can be used to clean things, and it can even be used to heal wounds! How does this relate to how we use words? We need to keep our words from hurting, destroying or overpowering others. Instead they should bless, and preserve

▼ *more...*

8

people's feelings. They should add graciousness, kindness, gentleness and compassion to conversations.

2. Be slow to speak

Know this, my beloved brothers: let every person be quick to hear, slow to speak, slow to anger.

—James 1:19

What does this mean? It means you should take your time in chatting, sharing and posting. Once you have shared something online, it's too late to take it back. Even if you delete it, people may have already seen it. And actually you can never really delete anything online. It's possible someone has copied it, shared it, snapchatted it, forwarded it to others. There are so many ways that your private words and photos can be shared with others who you never wanted to share them with. Take your time and think carefully before you push 'post'.

But what if someone has posted something that makes you angry? Look at the above verse again. It not only says that we are to be slow to be angry, but also that we are to be quick to listen. Maybe you need to go and talk to your parents about it and be quick to listen to their advice.

3. Zip your lips

When words are many, transgression is not lacking, but whoever restrains his lips is prudent.

—Proverbs 10:19

▼ *more...*

Transgression is another word for sin. The idea is that if we let loose with our tongue, it won't be long before we say things we shouldn't be saying. Choose your words carefully and keep a tight rein on how much you speak.

4. Watch the time

> [15] *Look carefully then how you walk, not as unwise but as wise,* [16] *making the most of the time, because the days are evil.*
>
> —Ephesians 5:15-16

Whenever we do something fun the time just whizzes away. Keep social media in perspective. While it can be fun to enjoy it for a bit, there are so many more things which are better to spend your time on. Enjoy 'real' activities, not just online ones. Ride your bike, paint a sunset, read a great book, play with your siblings, help make dinner, fold some laundry, hang out with your parents…. Keep it real and make the most of your time.

5. Invest in others

> *So then, as we have opportunity, let us do good to everyone, and especially those who are of the household of faith.*
>
> —Galatians 6:10

Being online can sometimes cause us to be like those horses who wear blinkers to keep them focussed. We can forget that those around us are real people with real needs as we have our heads down and eyes focussed on the screen. But the Bible commands all Christians to 'do good', especially to other Christians. It can be pretty hard to do good when our eyes are focussed on a screen.

▼ *more…*

6. Be an example

Let no one despise you for your youth, but set the believers an example in speech, in conduct, in love, in faith, in purity.

—1 Timothy 4:12

As I write, I am thinking about all sorts of terrible things that are happening online that young people are involved in. Much of it happens because of peer pressure – the pressure to be involved in something even though it might be wrong or inappropriate. Maybe inappropriate photos or videos are being shared. Or perhaps there is bullying, or the pressure to sign up for something that you don't want to do. Or it might be expressing attitudes which dishonour families and God. Whatever is going on, be an example. Sometimes the best example is to just walk away from whatever is going on. Other times we need to speak up. It's a hard thing to do, but we can follow the example of Jesus, who was always the best example for us to follow.

7. Know when to sign off

Blessed is the man who walks not in the counsel of the wicked, nor stands in the way of sinners, nor sits in the seat of scoffers.

—Psalm 1:1

If you are already allowed to use social media, you might find (as with any kind of friendship) that the influence, distraction or temptation you experience from it means that you need to stop using it. The Bible says that the person who does not walk with those who do not love God is blessed.

▼ *more...*

You could swap out the word 'blessed' for 'right' (from the original Hebrew of the word blessed). It is right to not walk in the way of those who don't love God. It honours God, it protects you and it is an example to others.

These are just some of the principles that Scripture has for us in our daily living that we can apply to our use of social media. They are important and precious principles because they are God's Words to us.

What have we Learnt about Social Media?

1. Social media is another way people communicate. It's instant, it can be fun— but it can also be dangerous.
2. Social media can become a problem when it causes us to treasure it above all else.
3. We can and should guard our hearts, making sure that Jesus is our treasure – not how many people like what we are sharing.
4. We using social media we should:
- Watch our words
- Be slow to speak
- Zip our lips
- Watch the time
- Invest in others
- Be an example
- Know when to sign off

When words are many, transgression is not lacking, but whoever restrains his lips is prudent.

—Proverbs 10:19

Study Questions

Let's look at the 'Zip your lips' principle.

Look at the verse below and list what sorts of wrong can come out of our mouths, and write a definition for each one:

For I fear that perhaps when I come I may find you not as I wish, and that you may find me not as you wish – that perhaps there may be quarrelling, jealousy, anger, hostility, slander, gossip, conceit, and disorder.

—2 Corinthians 12:20

Sometimes on social media, it's easy to feel a little more 'brave' or more 'independent from the household rules' than you would if you were talking to people in a face-to-face manner. And sometimes this means that things get written and posted that you would not say, if your parents were standing right there with you.

1. Have you ever posted something online that you regretted later?

   What effects did it have on your friendships/relationships?

   Why did you regret it?

   What have you learnt in this chapter that might encourage you now not to post such things again?

2. Imagine you were going to rewrite that sentence above (taken from a letter to the Corinthian church) but instead started it with:

▼ *more...*

14

"For I hope that when I come I will find you as I wish, and that you will find me as you wish – that perhaps there may be …."

3. What good/positive words would you want to complete the second half of the verse?

4. Why would you choose these words?

5. If you were to use social media, do these words describe what you hope your parents would find if they looked at your account?

6. What principles have you learnt from this chapter that will help you to achieve that?

7. What principles would you find the hardest to do?

8. Are there any changes that you can tell you already need to make in the way you use or think about social media? If yes, what?

Let's Pray Together

Dear God, thank you for technology, which allows us to keep in touch with friends all over the world, to have fun on different online sites, and to connect with people in a different way. With it, we know there are also some dangers. Please give us wisdom when we are online, protect us from those who would want to harm us and help us to keep ourselves safe. Please help us in our contacts with people to be wise, loving and true to you. May the principles we have read today be a guide as we make our way in the online world. Amen.

FOR WHERE YOUR TREASURE IS, THERE YOUR HEART WILL BE ALSO. (MATTHEW 6:21)

LET NO ONE DESPISE YOU FOR YOUR YOUTH, BUT SET THE BELIEVERS AN EXAMPLE IN SPEECH, IN CONDUCT, IN LOVE, IN FAITH, IN PURITY. (1 TIMOTHY 4:12)

BLESSED IS THE MAN WHO WALKS NOT IN THE COUNSEL OF THE WICKED, NOR STANDS IN THE WAY OF SINNERS, NOR SITS IN THE SEAT OF SCOFFERS. (PSALM 1:1)

MY ACTION PLAN

1.

2.

3.

4.

5.

What does the
Bible Say about...

Money?

 Think

 Ask

 Bible

A poor man was once carried to the gates of the home of a very rich man, and there he was laid. He had to be carried because he was so unwell, his body so covered in sores that he could not walk or even crawl to the gates himself.

He lay quietly at the gate, hoping that the rich man would take pity on him and send out a servant with some scraps of food from his table. And one day, he died. The rich man also died. But what happened next?

The poor man died and was carried by the angels to Abraham's side. The rich man also died and was buried, and in Hades, being in torment, he lifted up his eyes and saw Abraham far off and Lazarus at his side. And he called out, 'Father Abraham, have mercy on me, and send Lazarus to dip the end of his finger in water and cool my tongue, for I am in anguish in this flame.' But Abraham said, 'Child, remember that you in your lifetime received your good things, and Lazarus in like manner bad things; but now he is comforted here, and you are in anguish. And besides all this, between us and you a great chasm has been fixed, in order that those who would pass from here to you may not do so, and none may cross from there to us.' And he said, 'Then I beg you, father, to send him to my father's house – for I have five brothers – so that he may warn them, lest they also come into this place of torment.' But Abraham said, 'They have Moses and the Prophets; let them hear them.' And he said, 'No, father Abraham, but if someone goes to them from the dead, they will repent.' He said to him, 'If they do not hear Moses and the Prophets, neither will they be convinced if someone should rise from the dead.'

—Luke 16:22-31

Did You Know ...?

In some countries money is made from cloth, not paper – that's why it doesn't get ruined when it goes through the washing machine.

What a terribly sad story. The poor man, Lazarus, was in such a dreadful state while he was on earth and yet he was a godly man. He was saved by faith and his forever home was heaven. Look back and see how God even sent angels to bring Lazarus home to heaven. How wonderful for a man who had been ignored by men for so much of his life and left to die at the gates of a rich man's house. But then, the story got very sad. The rich man did not go to heaven. He went to a place called Hades – the place where man is forever separated from God. The rich man had no faith in God while on earth. It seems instead his faith was in his money.

What does it mean, to have faith in money? It means that the man believed he had everything he needed because he was rich enough to buy it. He foolishly depended on his money to provide him with the life that he wanted. But he did not understand that money does not buy forgiveness of sin or eternal life with the Creator God. Instead, his money became his god. A different rich man was once asked, 'How much money is enough?' He replied, 'Just a little more.' The desire to have money and make more of it, can turn money into a god to be served.

How do we know that the rich man served money? Luke chapter sixteen gives us some clues. When Lazarus was carried to the gates of the rich man and laid there – obviously in need of help – the rich man did nothing. He could have provided food – he himself feasted 'sumptuously' (luxurious, expensive and large). But he did not. He could have arranged for a doctor to help the man; he could certainly afford it. But he did not. In fact, he could have even offered the man a more comfortable place to lay, like a room in his own home. But he did none of these things.

Should he have helped the man? Was it his problem that there was a poor man laying at the gate to his home? Well, let's look at what the Bible says about the poor:

And he [John the Baptist] answered them, 'Whoever has two tunics is to share with him who has none, and whoever has food is to do likewise.'

—Luke 3:11

Whoever is generous to the poor lends to the LORD, and he will repay him for his deed.

—Proverbs 19:17

In all things I have shown you that by working hard in this way we must help the weak and remember the words of the Lord Jesus, how he himself said, 'It is more blessed to give than to receive.'

—Acts 20:35

If the rich man loved God, he would have helped Lazarus. Instead, he did all that gave himself pleasure and closed his eyes to anything else.

So what can we Learn about Money from this Story?

1. Money cannot get you to heaven

   Heaven is not a club where the rich can pay their membership and enter in. In fact, the Bible tells us the opposite.

   Blessed are the poor in spirit, for theirs is the kingdom of heaven.
   —Matthew 5:3

   This is not saying that poor people are blessed and will go to heaven – it's speaking of those who know they are poor in spirit. That means those who understand that they have no ability to 'save' themselves from their sin, nor present themselves as holy to God. Their spirits are not only poor, but are in debt – because the wages of sin is death. But Jesus came to pay the price of death through his own death on the cross, so that we don't have to. The poor in spirit receive Jesus' gift of life.

2. Riches are only for this lifetime

   When the rich man died, he left all his riches, his property and his fine clothes. In Hades, he had nothing, not even a servant to bring him water. But in his arrogance he still expected to be served (remember, he asked for Abraham to send Lazarus with some water to cool his tongue because he was in agony). Did he help Lazarus (who was no doubt in physical agony) when he lay at the gates to his home? No. He allowed himself to be blinded by his riches and treasure, even after he had lost it all. But there is a treasure that lasts.

   ▼ *more...*

Do not lay up for yourselves treasures on earth, where moth and rust destroy and where thieves break in and steal, but lay up for yourselves treasures in heaven, where neither moth nor rust destroys and where thieves do not break in and steal.

—Matthew 6:19-20

The Bible tells us not to be storing up treasures/wealth on earth where it does not last. Instead, we are to be storing up treasure in heaven. How do we do that?

Sell your possessions, and give to the needy. Provide yourselves with money bags that do not grow old, with a treasure in the heavens that does not fail, where no thief approaches and no moth destroys. For where your treasure is, there will your heart be also.

—Luke 12:33-34

When we show kindness to those who need it, we lay up for ourselves treasure in heaven. God does not want us to hold tightly to what we have, but rather to see it as a tool that we can use to bless those in need.

3. Riches can become a BIG distraction from the gospel

The rich man was so caught up in enjoying his money that he did not take time to think about the needs of his soul. Sure enough, his money was his treasure.

For where your treasure is, there your heart will be also.

—Matthew 6:21

But wait, there's more!

What other Principles can we Learn from Scripture?

It's perhaps easy to read the story of Lazarus and the rich man, and come to the conclusion that money is a terrible thing, that it's terrible to be rich and that we should hope to be poor! Is this a correct way to think about money? No, not at all. In fact, money can be a blessing. Let's look at some more principles to guide us in our thinking about money.

1. Money isn't the problem – but loving the money is

   For the love of money is a root of all kinds of evils. It is through this craving that some have wandered away from the faith and pierced themselves with many pangs.

   —1 Timothy 6:10

   Remember, money is just a 'thing'. It is neither alive nor dead, and it has no ability to make us selfish or generous. It is the attitude that we have towards money which is the issue. If we love money, then we can be sure our hearts will become hard to the gospel, to the needs of people, and to anything which might threaten our chances of having more money! Be careful to guard your heart from becoming a lover of money.

2. Being content with what we have protects us from becoming a lover of money

   Keep your life free from the love of money, and be content with what you have.

   —Hebrews 13:5a

▼ *more...*

24

Contentment. Do you know what that is? Is it a feeling, or is it an attitude? Well, perhaps it's both. You know the feeling after you have eaten a good meal? You're full, but not too full. You've enjoyed your meal, you know you don't need any more and you are… content. But sometimes we might think we need more anyway. Whether it's more money, more gadgets, more books, more clothes …. And this is where contentment needs to be an attitude.

Not that I am speaking of being in need, for I have learned in whatever situation I am to be content. I know how to be brought low, and I know how to abound. In any and every circumstance, I have learned the secret of facing plenty and hunger, abundance and need. I can do all things through him who strengthens me.

—Philippians 4:11-12

The apostle Paul talks about learning to be content. He says he has been in situations where he has had plenty and situations where he has been in need of more – but he learnt to be content with what he had. How? Paul knew that he could do all things, and face all situations, through Christ, who gave him strength. Contentment comes through trusting Christ to meet all your needs.

3. Everything we have comes from God.

God gives us both ability and intelligence to earn money, so ultimately wealth comes from God.

Both riches and honour come from you, and you rule over all. In your hand are power and might, and in your hand it is to make great and to give strength to all. And now we thank you, our God and praise your glorious name.

—1 Chronicles 29:12-13

▼ *more...*

4. We are not to worry about money

And he [Jesus] said to his disciples, 'Therefore I tell you, do not be anxious about your life, what you will eat, nor about your body, what you will put on. For life is more than food, and the body more than clothing. Consider the ravens: they neither sow nor reap, they have neither storehouse nor barn, and yet God feeds them. Of how much more value are you than the birds?

—Luke 12:22-24

We are to be careful with the money that God has provided for us – not using it carelessly – and then we are to trust God to provide all of our needs, without worrying.

5. Money is to be used for the good of others

They [the rich] are to do good, to be rich in good works, to be generous and ready to share.

—1 Timothy 6:18

We are to give generously to those who are in need of help. Think about the phrase 'good works'. From what you know of the Lord and His teachings in the Bible, what would He consider to be good works? Perhaps things like the care of orphans and widows, the provision of food and clothing for those who need it, the opportunity for partnering alongside those who share the gospel with unbelievers and those who teach the Word to the church. I'm sure you can think of others too.

WHOEVER IS GENEROUS TO THE POOR LENDS TO THE LORD, AND HE WILL REPAY HIM FOR HIS DEED. (PROVERBS 19:17)

IN ALL THINGS I HAVE SHOWN YOU THAT BY WORKING HARD IN THIS WAY WE MUST HELP THE WEAK AND REMEMBER THE WORDS OF THE LORD JESUS, HOW HE HIMSELF SAID, 'IT IS MORE BLESSED TO GIVE THAN TO RECEIVE.' (ACTS 20:35)

Study Questions

1. *Better is a dry morsel with quiet than a house full of feasting with strife.*
   —Proverbs 17:1

   This proverb tells us that a peaceful home with basic food is better than a home with feasting but trouble. Why do you think that is?

2. *Better a poor person who walks in his integrity than one who is crooked in speech and is a fool.*
   —Proverbs 19:1

   Integrity means someone who is honest and trustworthy in all that they do. This proverb compares someone who is poor but has integrity with someone who uses lies and dishonest words to make money.

   Why do you think people could be dishonest if it means they can make some money?

   If you knew someone who was doing this, how would you use the above proverb to talk to them about it?

3. *A good name is to be chosen rather than great riches, and favour is better than silver or gold.*
   —Proverbs 22:1

   What does it mean to have a 'good name'? Why is that better than riches? Does this mean that having money is bad? Why not? What is the most important thing – the good name or the riches?

▼ *more...*

28

Let's Pray Together

Dear God, thank you for what we have learnt about money. We know that the ability to work and earn money comes from you and we are grateful. We also know that money is not a bad thing, but if we let it become our treasure above all else, that is wrong. Please help us to keep you as our treasure, and to keep a right view of how we earn and use money. Please help us to grow to be those who use money for your glory and your Kingdom. Thank you for providing all of our needs, and more. Amen.

KEEP YOUR LIFE FREE FROM THE LOVE OF MONEY, AND BE CONTENT WITH WHAT YOU HAVE. (HEBREWS 13:5A)

BOTH RICHES AND HONOUR COME FROM YOU, AND YOU RULE OVER ALL. IN YOUR HAND ARE POWER AND MIGHT, AND IN YOUR HAND IT IS TO MAKE GREAT AND TO GIVE STRENGTH TO ALL. AND NOW WE THANK YOU, OUR GOD, AND PRAISE YOUR GLORIOUS NAME. (1 CHRONICLES 29:12-13)

MY ACTION PLAN

1.

2.

3.

4.

5.

What does the
Bible Say about...

Authority?

Think

Ask

Bible

Do you know what a centurion is? A centurion was a soldier of Rome, but not just any old soldier: he was the commander of 100 Roman soldiers. He would have started off as a basic soldier, and after years of hard work and outstanding courage, skill and bravery in battle, he would have been promoted to the role of centurion. There were sixty centurions in each Roman legion (that's 6,000 soldiers), with senior officers in charge of the legions. The centurion had men who were in authority over him and men who served under him, for the sake of serving their country and king.

One day, as Jesus was entering a place called Capernaum, he was approached by a Roman centurion. Don't forget, it was Roman soldiers who would later take Jesus away to face His death, but today the centurion was more concerned about someone else.

When he entered Capernaum, a centurion came forward to him, appealing to him, 'Lord, my servant is lying paralyzed at home, suffering terribly.' And he said to him, 'I will come and heal him.' But the centurion replied, 'Lord, I am not worthy to have you come under my roof, but only say the word, and my servant will be healed. For I am a man under authority, with soldiers under me. And I say to one, "Go," and he goes, and to another, "Come," and he comes, and to my servant, "Do this," and he does it.'

—Matthew 8:5-9

This is an amazing situation for a number of reasons, one being that the Romans hated the Jews and yet this centurion approaches Jesus for His help! However, we see that the centurion clearly understands what authority is. He even tells Jesus that he himself is a man who is under authority and that he then also has authority over others. Do you know what authority is? And why would the centurion be talking about authority in this situation instead of just 'healing' as Jesus said?

Did You Know ...?

A Roman soldier who disobeyed orders and put others lives at risk would be punished by pain and possible death!

Let's first look at what authority is. It means the power to give and enforce orders. If I asked you right now to give me an example of people in authority today, you might say police officers. You would be correct. Police officers enforce the law so that everyone can be kept safe, enabling our society to function in a fair and orderly way.

You might notice that authority has a reason and this reason is often to maintain order. Order enables function. That means having something in order makes a situation or thing work well.

For example, I like to keep my kitchen in order so that I can work in it without having to first clean up the mess from the last meal. So, we have rules in our house that the dishes are done, things are cleared away and counters wiped down after every meal. It means that we are then ready to use the kitchen at any time again without having to backtrack and clean up from last time. Having an orderly kitchen means that we can *function* as we should in the kitchen.

Imagine if the centurion neglected to use his authority to keep his soldiers in order, instead allowing them to do whatever they wanted. Probably many of them would never turn up for battle, and if they did they might just do whatever they wanted instead of moving forward together as a team. It would be chaos, and certainly on the battlefield there would be no victory. So the centurion gives orders. He tells his soldiers where to be, how to fight and what armour and weapon to use, all because he knows how soldiers should function best and how to order them to carry it out.

It's easy to see where the need for authority comes from, isn't it? If there are no rules in society, there would be chaos.

It was way back at the beginning, when order and authority were set in place. The beginning? Yep, the very beginning.

> *Then God said, 'Let us make man in our image, after our likeness. And let them have dominion over the fish of the sea and over the birds of the heavens and over the livestock and over all the earth and over every creeping thing that creeps on the earth.'*
>
> —Genesis 1:26

The above verse is taken from the creation account. You can see that God had a plan, which He carried out. He would make man (man and woman) and He would give them dominion (authority) over all the creatures. God was setting order in His new creation. He was showing that animals and man are not equal by placing man in authority over the creatures.

Then God continued on in establishing order.

> *Then the Lord God said, 'It is not good that the man should be alone; I will make him a helper fit for him.'*
>
> —Genesis 2:18

God gave Adam a wife. See how God calls Adam's wife a helper? That gives the clue of her role in the marriage. Adam is the head and the wife is the helper. Adam is not better than his wife, Eve; they just have a different job in the marriage. God established order in marriage in this way.

Where else did God establish order? Perhaps you might be thinking of the family. God established order by giving parents authority over their children.

Children, obey your parents in the Lord, for this is right.

—Ephesians 6:1

God put people in positions of authority for our good. But the big question is, is there someone who is in charge of *everything*? That takes us back to the Roman centurion's visit to Jesus.

When he [Jesus] entered Capernaum, a centurion came forward to him, appealing to him, 'Lord, my servant is lying paralyzed at home, suffering terribly.' And he said to him, 'I will come and heal him.' But the centurion replied, 'Lord, I am not worthy to have you come under my roof, but only say the word, and my servant will be healed. For I too am a man under authority, with soldiers under me. And I say to one, "Go", and he goes, and to another, "Come" and he comes, and to my servant, "Do this", and he does it.' When Jesus heard this, he marvelled and said to those who followed him, 'Truly, I tell you, with no one in Israel have I found such faith. I tell you, many will come from east and west and recline at table with Abraham, Isaac, and Jacob in the kingdom of heaven, while the sons of the kingdom will be thrown into the outer darkness. In that place there will be weeping and gnashing of teeth.' And to the centurion Jesus said, 'Go; let it be done for you as you have believed.' And the servant was healed at that very moment.

—Matthew 8:5-13

The centurion comes to Jesus, concerned about his servant, who is suffering terribly and lying paralyzed at home. Jesus talks about healing, but the centurion talks about authority. Jesus is amazed. Then Jesus talks about heaven and about hell and faith. Suddenly the servant is healed. Do you understand what has happened? Let me tell you.

The centurion understands who Jesus is. He is not just a carpenter, or a Jew or even a teacher. No, the centurion understands that Jesus is the Son of God. He knows that Jesus has authority over all things. Everything. Not just people, but circumstances, sicknesses, death and life. Every single thing you or I could think of is ultimately under the authority of Jesus.

And Jesus came and said to them, 'All authority in heaven and on earth has been given to me.'

—Matthew 28:18

What was the centurion doing talking about Jesus' authority? The centurion was placing himself under the rightful authority of Jesus because the centurion was a Christian. He believed Jesus was the Son of God and he willingly submitted his own life to Jesus! He knew Jesus did not need to come to his house to heal the man. Jesus had authority over that sickness and could heal him right then and there. And He did!

Do you believe, like the centurion, that Jesus has authority over all things? Jesus' response to the centurion's faith was to tell others who were standing and listening what would happen for those who have faith in Him, and those who don't. And then, in great compassion, and proving Himself to be God's Son, Jesus healed the servant.

There is so much we can learn from the centurion. He was a man who came as the one in authority over the servant, and yet he made clear that he placed himself under the authority of his Lord, Jesus.

As the one in authority, the centurion …

1. WAS HUMBLE. He came to Jesus and called Him 'Lord'. The very title of 'Lord' places a person in a higher rank. He also told Jesus

that he was not worthy to have Jesus come to his home, showing great humility. Nor did he send another servant to find Jesus – he went himself.

2. WAS COMPASSIONATE. He did not have to care for his servant in this way and in fact it would probably have been unusual for him to do so. If a servant was unable to work due to sickness, they were often sent away.

3. WAS KIND. The centurion went out of his way to serve a man whose job it was to serve him! And he didn't make a small effort; he did the very best he could for his servant by going straight to Jesus.

As the one under the authority of Jesus, the centurion…

1. WAS HUMBLE. He came to Jesus knowing that only Jesus could help. Neither did he consider himself, a centurion, worthy to have Jesus in his home.

2. WAS WILLING. The centurion was happy to be told what to do.

3. WAS A WITNESS. He was an example to those who were standing and watching this situation of what it is to believe in Jesus.

Isn't it interesting that regardless of whether the centurion was in a position of authority over his soldiers, or under the authority of his Lord, he was humble? When you think about those who you might have authority over, perhaps at a club or in a sports team – do you think you would be described as humble? What about those who have authority over you, (like a teacher, coach or your parents) – would they describe you as responding with humility?

But wait, there's more!

What other Principles can we Learn from Scripture?

Bible

There were once three young men who lived in Jerusalem and who served God. King Nebuchadnezzar, from Babylon, came to Jerusalem and besieged it, capturing the people including these three young men. They were then chosen to go and be trained up for the king's service. This was all against their will. And yet God had a plan for these young men who loved Him.

King Nebuchadnezzar believed he was under no authority but his own, and he did whatever pleased him. We get a hint of that in the way he took captive a whole city of people to build his own kingdom and wealth. Later, he had a golden idol made and he ordered all the people to bow down to it.

And the herald proclaimed aloud, 'You are commanded, O peoples, nations, and languages, that when you hear the sound of the horn, pipe, lyre, trigon, harp, bagpipe, and every kind of music, you are to fall down and worship the golden image that King Nebuchadnezzar has set up. And whoever does not fall down and worship shall immediately be cast into a burning fiery furnace.'

—Daniel 3:4-6

The young men whom the King had taken into his household had already made a name for themselves as wise men.

▼ *more...*

And in every matter of wisdom and understanding about which the king inquired of them, he found them ten times better than all the magicians and enchanters that were in all his kingdom.

—Daniel 1:20

We know that they served God and yet the King ordered them to bow down and worship an idol. What did they do? They refused to bow.

Then Nebuchadnezzar in furious rage commanded that Shadrach, Meshach, and Abednego be brought. So they brought these men before the king. Nebuchadnezzar answered and said to them, 'Is it true, O Shadrach, Meshach, and Abednego, that you do not serve my gods or worship the golden image that I have set up? Now if you are ready when you hear the sound of the horn, pipe, lyre, trigon, harp, bagpipe, and every kind of music, to fall down and worship the image that I have made, well and good. But if you do not worship, you shall immediately be cast into a burning fiery furnace. And who is the god who will deliver you out of my hands?' Shadrach, Meshach, and Abednego answered and said to the king, 'O Nebuchadnezzar, we have no need to answer you in this matter. If this be so, our God whom we serve is able to deliver us from the burning fiery furnace, and he will deliver us out of your hand, O king. But if not, be it known to you, O king, that we will not serve your gods or worship the golden image that you have set up.'

—Daniel 3:13-18

Hmmm. Did these boys do the right thing? Their response reminds me of the apostle Peter, who was told that he was not allowed to teach about Jesus.

▼ *more...*

But Peter and the apostles answered, 'We must obey God rather than men.

—Acts 5:29

What is Peter talking of here? Jesus had told the apostles that they were to go and preach the gospel regardless of persecution, and that is exactly what Peter and the apostles did.

But what about these young men who were facing Nebuchadnezzar's fiery furnace? They knew that the first two of the Ten Commandments applied to them in this very situation:

You shall have no other gods before me. You shall not make for yourself a carved image, or any likeness of anything that is in heaven above, or that is on the earth beneath, or that is in the water under the earth. You shall not bow down to them or serve them.

—Deuteronomy 5:7-9a

Just as the apostle Peter did, these young men also chose to obey God rather than man. This is an important truth regarding authority. God created authority to maintain order. Man can sometimes use authority for his own glory or selfish purposes, requiring that others disobey God in order to keep man's law. But the Bible is clear. In times such as these we are to obey God rather than man. And as we see with these brave young men, at times the consequences are dire. But the Bible has another answer to that.

▼ *more...*

We are not to fear the consequences of obeying God rather than man. He is in complete control over that situation, and while it might be a very hard thing for us to do, God will be honoured.

And do not fear those who kill the body but cannot kill the soul. Rather fear him who can destroy both soul and body in hell. Are not two sparrows sold for a penny? And not one of them will fall to the ground apart from your Father. But even the hairs of your head are all numbered. Fear not, therefore; you are of more value than many sparrows. So everyone who acknowledges me before men, I also will acknowledge before my Father who is in heaven, but whoever denies me before men, I also will deny before my Father who is in heaven.

—Matthew 10:28-33

So, what happened to the young men facing the fiery furnace? Well, God saved them. You need to read the rest of Daniel chapter three to get all the details, but they were honoured by God for their courage in obeying Him rather than the selfish king. Does God always step in and perform a miracle like He did for these young men? No, He doesn't. We need to remember this life is temporary. It's not forever. But for those who obey God on this earth, there is great reward waiting for them in heaven.

What did we Learn about Authority?

Ask

- God, who has authority over all things, created authority to maintain order.

- We are to be humble towards those in authority over us, as a witness to the God we serve.

- We are to be humble towards those we have authority over, as a witness to the God we serve.

- God has ultimate authority over all things and all people

- We are to obey God rather than man.

- Man can use authority for his own selfish purposes, sometimes requiring people to disobey God.

- God is honoured when we obey Him rather than man.

Study Questions

Think

Shadrach, Meshach, and Abednego answered and said to the king, 'O Nebuchadnezzar, we have no need to answer you in this matter. If this be so, our God whom we serve is able to deliver us from the burning fiery furnace, and he will deliver us out of your hand, O king. But if not, be it known to you, O king, that we will not serve your gods or worship the golden image that you have set up.'

—Daniel 3:13-18

1. When Shadrach, Meshach and Abednego were called to the king to explain why they had not bowed to his golden image, they answered in a very respectful but truthful manner. Imagine you were in a situation where you knew it was wrong for you to obey someone. What have you learnt from Shadrach and his friends' response to the king, as an example for you to follow?

2. Why was Nebuchadnezzar so furious with the young men for choosing not to bow down to the idol? Did it affect Nebuchadnezzar in any way or was it because he was not getting his own way?

3. When the young men refused to submit to Nebuchadnezzar's authority, he wanted them murdered. Compare the character traits and attitudes of Nebuchadnezzar with the centurion we read about earlier. What are the differences? Who do you think people would be more willing to follow? Why?

4. Who is in authority over you at the moment? Are there any changes you feel you need to make to your own responses towards people in authority over/under you? If yes, what?

▼ *more...*

44

Let's Pray Together

Dear God, thank you for the example of the centurion. He was humble when he came to Jesus because he knew that Jesus was the one in authority over all things. Please help us to be humble in submitting to Jesus in our lives. May we also follow the example of the young men thrown into the fire. May we be respectful, courageous and true to you, whether people are in authority over us, or if we are in authority over others. Amen.

AND JESUS CAME AND SAID TO THEM, 'ALL AUTHORITY IN HEAVEN AND ON EARTH HAS BEEN GIVEN TO ME.' (MATTHEW 28:18)

BUT PETER AND THE APOSTLES ANSWERED, 'WE MUST OBEY GOD RATHER THAN MEN.' (ACTS 5:29)

MY ACTION PLAN

1.

2.

3.

4.

5.

What does the
Bible Say about...

Gaming, TV
& Movies?

 Think

 Ask

 Bible

I heard some interesting facts on the news recently. They said that children between the ages of 8 and 15 are spending, on average, three hours a day playing video games, and five hours a day watching television. I don't know how they gathered this information, but if they are correct it is shocking to think that some children are spending eight hours a day in front of a screen. That's not even including any time that is spent online for school-related activities.

Let's look at it another way:

Number of hours in a day:	24 hours
Recommended hours of sleep for 8-15 year olds:	8-12 hours
Hours spent each day on education/school:	6 hours
Supposed number of hours per day in front of a screen:	8 hours
Total:	22+ hours

Hmmm – something doesn't add up, does it? Where is the time for eating, showering, reading, playing, being with family and friends, helping with chores, doing homework, exercising and a million other things? When we think about all the activities that we need to fit into each day, it's hard to imagine that someone could really be in front of a screen for that long. Or is it?

Did You Know ...?

Watching a screen at night can make it hard to sleep because the bright lights don't allow your body to wind down and prepare to sleep.

So, what then does the Bible say about playing video games? Actually, like many of the other topics that we've looked it, the Bible says nothing about it. Not one single verse. Obviously, the kids back in Old Testament days, and in Jesus' day, didn't have video games. Nor did they need them. David killed a real giant with a slingshot and stone. Daniel was thrown into a den of man-eating lions – and survived! And there was a group of men that really did try to build a real tower to reach heaven!

However, even though there are no verses in the Bible about gaming, we know that the Bible has principles to guide us in all of our life. Here are some principles to consider when we think about video games.

1. Do not love violence.

   The LORD tests the righteous, but his soul hates the wicked and the one who loves violence.

   —Psalm 11:5

   It seems like many video games and even T.V. programmes are centred around violence. God created life and it is precious. Be careful of playing games that make life unimportant, or that make harming or killing others pleasurable or fun.

2. Do not love money.

   Provide yourselves with money bags that do not grow old, with a treasure in the heavens that does not fail, where no thief approaches and no moth destroys.

   —Luke 12:33b

   Games that aim to store up wealth and television programmes that focus on money tempt our hearts in very real ways! Many games provide opportunities to earn 'fake' money and purchase 'fake' things. Be careful that your heart does not start to long for the real money, and the real possessions. Be content with what you have.

3. Don't do things/watch things on a screen that you know to be wrong in real life.

Take no part in the unfruitful works of darkness, but instead expose them. For it is shameful even to speak of the things that they do in secret. But when anything is exposed by the light, it becomes visible.
—Ephesians 5:11-13

Unfruitful works of darkness could mean all sorts of things, couldn't it? Witchcraft and sorcery, wrong relationships, attitudes and character traits that dishonour your parents and God; these are just some of what we might see on a screen. But the Bible tells us to be very careful about what we allow ourselves to see. Look at this verse.

'The eye is the lamp of the body. So, if your eye is healthy, your whole body will be full of light.'
—Matthew 6:22

This means that what you allow yourself to see or watch will influence what you think. If we focus on Christ and His truths, His light enables us to see situations clearly and make wise decisions. But if we allow our eyes (and therefore our minds) to dwell on things that are dark (sinful), our minds will be pulled more and more towards sin.

4. Do not look only for pleasure.

Whoever loves pleasure will be a poor man.
—Proverbs 21:17a

Now wait a minute … before you start worrying that the Bible is telling you not to enjoy yourself, let me reassure you. This verse is not saying that we can't have fun. But it is saying that someone whose chief aim in life is to have fun will be poor, because working to earn their living is often not as much fun. But what does this mean for the student who does not yet need to work to earn money? It's a warning for you to make sure that you do not develop bad habits. Make sure that you are just as willing to do the chores and tasks that are not as pleasurable, so that you do not become someone who only looks for pleasure.

5. Do not be conformed to this world's ways.

Do not be conformed to this world, but be transformed by the renewal of your mind, that by testing you may discern what is the will of God, what is good and acceptable and perfect.

—Romans 12:2

What does this mean? It means that you don't need to follow the crowds. There will always be games or movies that are very popular, but for various reasons would be unwise for you to play or see. For Christians, honouring the Lord with our choices is more important than fitting in with others. To be conformed means that you become like something/someone else. Choose not to be like the world, but choose to be like Jesus instead.

6. Do not imitate evil.

Beloved, do not imitate evil, but imitate good. Whoever does good is from God; whoever does evil has not seen God.

—3 John 1:11

This is pretty clear, isn't it? Be careful of the video games you choose to play and what you can do with them.

7. Do not mock God.

Do not be deceived: God is not mocked, for whatever one sows, that will he also reap.

—Galatians 6:7

These verses are a clear warning to us. The first statement says that God cannot be mocked. This means that no one can say that they love God but live and behave as if they don't. The second part of the verse tells us why. What we sow, we reap. If we sow (plant) lettuce seeds in the garden, what do we expect to see growing there soon after? Cucumbers or roses perhaps? No, of course not! We would expect to see lettuces. So, whatever we plant (sow) in our lives, that is what will see grow (reap). Consider carefully the video games you play or the movies you watch. Are they planting into your life attitudes, behaviours, examples, habits and lifestyles which will help you to grow into a mature Christian?

8. Do not forget to do good.

So then, as we have opportunity, let us do good to everyone, and especially to those who are of the household of faith.

—Galatians 6:10

If the statistics that we read earlier are anywhere near correct, then a lot of people are stuck in front of a screen focussing on themselves, instead of serving and caring for others. Don't forget to lift your eyes from the screen to see what good you can do for those around you.

9. Do not forget your parents.

Children, obey your parents in the Lord, for this is right. Honour your father and mother (this is the first commandment with a promise), that it may go well with you and that you may live long in the land.

—Ephesians 6:1-3

I wonder how many arguments occur around the world, between parents and children, over video games, television and movies. Arguments over how much time has been spent in front of the screen, what is actually happening on the screen, how much it costs, how many chores are left undone. I'm sure you could add a few more too. This might even seem a normal thing to many families – something that they just expect to happen every day now. But it shouldn't be. The Bible is very clear in requiring children to honour and obey their parents. To honour does not mean to bow down in front of. It means to make sure your attitudes and responses towards them are respectful, showing them that you understand that you are under their authority in the home. And obviously, obedience is a willingness to quickly and cheerfully obey house rules. The Bible goes on to say that those who keep these commands will be blessed. I guess that also must mean that those who are disrespectful and disobedient to their parents will not be blessed.

But wait, there's more.

What other Principles can we Learn from Scripture?

Bible

So we have looked at a number of 'do nots'. But here's one that says 'do'.

Do use your time wisely.

> *Look carefully then how you walk, not as unwise but as wise, making the best use of time, because the days are evil.*
>
> —Ephesians 5:15-16

The word 'walk' doesn't actually mean 'one foot in front of the other'. It is talking about how you live your life. We might even call our Christian life 'our walk with the Lord' because we are journeying through this life here on earth until we reach our final destination of heaven. The Bible tells us to walk wisely, making the best use of our time. Now, again, this isn't saying that we can't or shouldn't spend time doing fun things. But it is cautioning us to keep a good track of how we are spending our time. Maybe you are wondering what the verse above means when it says 'the best use of time'. It means activities that we should be doing, things that, if left undone, are going to cause problems. This might mean your homework, your chores, exercising, studying your Bible, time in prayer, serving others, showing love to your siblings by playing with them – all sorts of things that couldn't be considered wasting time. If these 'best' things are not getting the most of your time spent on them and the 'pleasure' things (like video games or movies) are, then you need to ask yourself if you are making the

▼ *more...*

best use of your time. Remember, this life is temporary. It's unlikely that on your death bed you will look back over your life and wish that you had spent more time in front of a screen. But it is possible that you will look back and wish you had invested your life more in something that would have great value towards your heavenly future, or the legacy that you left behind.

What did we Learn about Gaming, Television and Movies?

Ask

- There are only twenty-four hours in the day and some people are spending a third of that time in front of a screen.

- Principles to guide us:

  - do not love violence

  - do not love money

  - do not watch/do things on a screen that you know to be wrong

  - do not always seek after pleasure

  - do not be conformed to this world

  - do not imitate evil

  - do not mock God

  - do not forget to do good

  - do not forget your parents

  - do use your time wisely

Study Questions

Look carefully then how you walk, not as unwise but as wise, making the best use of time, because the days are evil.

—Ephesians 5:15-16

1. See if you can write out an average day or week of all the various activities you do, and how much time you spend on each activity. Don't forget to include sleeping, eating, school etc.

   - Are you surprised by how much time you spend on some activities? What ones?

   - How many hours a day do you think you spend in front of a video game/television screen?

   - How does this compare to everything else you are doing? (is it more or less time?)

   - Are there any activities that you feel should be on your list, but aren't? If so, what? Why are they not there now?

   - Are there any changes that you would like to make to your schedule so that you make the best use of your time? If yes, how could you do that?

The LORD tests the righteous, but his soul hates the wicked and the one who loves violence.

—Psalm 11:5

▼ *more...*

2. Why do you think games/movies with violence are so popular?

- How do you think they affect the way we think about real life violence?

Whoever loves pleasure will be a poor man.

—Proverbs 21:17a

3. What are the dangers in always looking to do things that bring us pleasure?

- If we are continually seeking after pleasure, what attitudes are we in danger of developing towards; others, work/chores, serving others who need help?

Children, obey your parents in the Lord, for this is right. 'Honour your father and mother' (this is the first commandment with a promise), 'that it may go well with you and that you may live long in the land.'

—Ephesians 6:1-3

4. What do you think causes arguments with parents over screen time?

- Using the command in Ephesians 6 (above), what would be the best way to sort out these arguments?

▼ *more...*

Let's Pray Together

Dear God, thank you for the way that you have created us, with abilities that are so clever and with skills and talents that we can use to create, entertain, encourage and bless others. As we have looked at principles to guide us in our use of video games and television/movies, we can see that as well as fun, there is also some potential for them to be a problem. Please give us wisdom to do the things that are good for us and to turn from the things that would harm us. Please also give parents wisdom as they seek to guide in this. Amen.

THE LORD TESTS THE RIGHTEOUS, BUT HIS SOUL HATES THE WICKED AND THE ONE WHO LOVES VIOLENCE. (PSALM 11:5)

LOOK CAREFULLY THEN HOW YOU WALK, NOT AS UNWISE BUT AS WISE, MAKING THE BEST USE OF TIME, BECAUSE THE DAYS ARE EVIL. (EPHESIANS 5:15-16)

MY ACTION PLAN

1.

2.

3.

4.

5.

What does the Bible Say about...

Knowing God's Will?

 Think

 Ask

 Bible

Mary was a young girl who lived in Nazareth. She was probably in her early to mid-teens and she lived at home with her family. Her parents seemed to be godly people because Mary knew the Scriptures. And like many other girls her age, Mary was engaged to be married.

Engaged to be married, and so young? Yes, it was normal for girls of this time to be engaged or married at a young age. I wonder if you've guessed exactly who this girl is? She is the young woman who became the mother of Jesus.

So, life was going along as Mary and her parents would have expected. Until, that is, Mary received a visit from an angel!

In the sixth month the angel Gabriel was sent from God to a city of Galilee named Nazareth, to a virgin betrothed to a man whose name was Joseph, of the house of David. And the virgin's name was Mary. And he came to her and said, 'Greetings, O favoured one, the Lord is with you!' But she was greatly troubled at the saying, and tried to discern what sort of greeting this might be. And the angel said to her, 'Do not be afraid, Mary, for you have found favour with God. And behold, you will conceive in your womb and bear a son, and you shall call his name Jesus. He will be great and will be called the Son of the Most High. And the Lord God will give to him the throne of his father David, and he will reign over the house of Jacob forever, and of his kingdom there will be no end.'

—Luke 1:26-33

Wow! How must that have felt? Not only to be visited by an angel, but to be given news that must have sent her head spinning! A baby?! An unmarried woman having a baby? This was surely not good news? Mary knew that being pregnant before she was married could really mean trouble. Her fiancé could call off the wedding. Her parents would be shamed. And she – well, she could be thrown out of her home or even put to death. At first, Mary didn't understand how she, an unmarried woman, could have a baby. But the angel told her that the Holy Spirit's power had come upon her and therefore the baby in her womb was the Son of God.

Did You Know ...?

It is better to be poor walking in the will of God than to be rich walking outside of the will of God.

If Mary was in shock over the visit from an angel and the news that she was to have a baby, she was surely overwhelmed by this new information: The baby was the Son of the Most High God.

Take a minute to think this through. How do you think people would respond to Mary telling them this? Would they think she was lying? Or maybe they would think she was crazy! Certainly there would be many who would think she was being blasphemous (extremely disrespectful towards God).

And yet, Mary's response makes sense. God would not have chosen just anyone to bring His Beloved Son into the world. He chose a mature, godly and faith-filled young woman who loved and trusted Him.

And Mary said, 'Behold I am the servant of the Lord; let it be to me according to your word.' And the angel departed from her.

—Luke 1:38

Mary basically said, 'I am God's servant. Whatever God has planned for my life; I will accept it.'

Then the angel left her. This is interesting. The angel left because he didn't have to do anything more. No calming a hysterical young woman, no talking her into accepting what God had planned for her life. Nothing. He had delivered his message, she had believed it and received it. Then he left.

Even later on, when things surely became more difficult as she shared the news with her family and her fiancé, her response was calm, mature and honouring to the Lord.

> And Mary said, 'My soul magnifies the Lord, and my spirit rejoices in God my Saviour, for he has looked on the humble estate of his servant. For behold, from now on all generations will call me blessed; for he who is mighty has done great things for me, and holy is his name. And his mercy is for those who fear him from generation to generation.
>
> —Luke 1:46-50

Mary was not looking for God's will when the angel visited her. She was already 'in it'. What do I mean by that? Mary was living a life that honoured her parents, that honoured her God and she loved and trusted in Him. Then God made a change to how she thought her life was going to look. A huge change. Probably a frightening change. And certainly the change bought with it a lot of unknowns. Mary had no idea how things would turn out for her. But she knew one thing for sure. God had done this, and it was His will for her life. So, she accepted it, praised Him for it and carried on.

Sometimes we can make a big deal out of finding out God's will for our lives. It almost turns into a guessing game, trying to figure out what God wants us to do with our lives. We worry that we might somehow miss the thing He wants us to do. But that's not how God works. It's a whole lot simpler.

Ask yourself the following questions:

- Have I believed in Jesus as my Saviour, repented of my sin and put my trust in God?

- Am I trying my best (with the Lord's help) to live a life that honours Him, by obeying Him?

- Am I growing in my Christian life by regularly reading my Bible, and spending time in prayer? Am I seeing the 'fruit of the Spirit' in my life? (See Galatians 5:22)

If you can say yes to those questions, then guess what? You are 'in God's will' for your life!

But wait, there's more!

What other Principles can we Learn from Scripture?

Bible

Now I can already hear that some of you will be saying, 'But how do I know what job I should have when I grow up?' 'How do I know if I am meant to be a missionary, or a builder, or a doctor or a plumber?'

These are all good questions. A time is coming in your life when you'll have a lot of decisions to make that will have an impact on your future. But don't worry about it; God knows you have all of this ahead of you and has given some principles to guide you in it.

▼ *more...*

God's Will for Your Life

1. To be saved

    This is good, and it is pleasing in the sight of God our Saviour, who desires all people to be saved and to come to the knowledge of the truth.

    —1 Timothy 2:3-4

    We've talked about this before, but it is the most important part of God's will for you. You cannot know God's will for your future if you are not saved. This is God's will for you. So... are you?

2. Love God and others

    And he answered, 'You shall love the Lord your God with all your heart and with all your soul and with all your strength and with all your mind, and your neighbour as yourself.'

    —Luke 10:27

    As we have seen many times already, it is so easy for us to lose our focus and be distracted from God by other things or other people. The first part of this verse calls you to love God with everything you are. Remember, love is an action, not a feeling. Live in a way that puts your love for God as a clear priority in all you do, turning from sin and walking in obedience to Him.

    The second part of this verse calls us to love our neighbour as we love ourselves. We tend to take very good care of ourselves, don't we? We eat, sleep, exercise, play, enjoy time with people we love, plan enjoyable things and try to make sure we don't miss out on doing fun stuff. God wants us to show that same kind of care and love to those around us. Be kind, understanding, patient, compassionate and generous to others.

▼ *more...*

3. Trust the Lord

    Trust in the LORD with all your heart, and do not lean on your own understanding, In all your ways acknowledge him, and he will make straight your paths.

    —Proverbs 3:5-6

    This verse tells us not to depend on our own wisdom, but to depend on and trust God. God is in control over all things and we can trust Him. When we trust Him and depend on Him, our paths become clear in His time.

4. Don't be anxious

    Do not be anxious about anything, but in everything by prayer and supplication with thanksgiving let your requests be known to God. And the peace of God, which passes all understanding, will guard your hearts and minds in Christ Jesus.

    —Philippians 4:6-7

    Don't worry – instead pray, asking the Lord to help you with decisions and choices.

5. Be who God made you to be

    Now there are varieties of gifts, but the same Spirit, and there are varieties of service, but the same Lord; and there are varieties of activities, but it is the same God who empowers them all in everyone.

    —1 Corinthians 12:4-6

    God has made us all uniquely. The gifts, abilities and talents He has given you are probably quite different to what He has given to your siblings or your friends. The things you are good at doing make you no better than someone else who is good

▼ more...

at other things. And likewise, if you are bottom of your English class, that makes you no less valuable than the person who gets top marks. God has given you special abilities and gifts so that you can use them for His glory.

6.   Whatever you do, make sure it is to the glory of God

So, whether you eat or drink, or whatever you do, do all to the glory of God.

—1 Corinthians 10:31

Whatever you do with your life, God's will is that you do it for His glory. Not for your glory, or for someone else's, but for God's.

But how does this help for when you start thinking about future jobs and education? If you are great at maths but can't hold a tune when you sing, it's pretty unlikely that you will have song writing in your future. Likewise, if you are creative but science is not your thing, you probably won't end up in a science lab for your job. God has made you just as you are for a reason. This doesn't mean that you shouldn't work hard at something you find difficult – you should always work hard and do your best because that brings God glory. But it does mean that the things you are good at and love doing are perhaps a good starting place for thinking about future jobs.

What did we Learn about Knowing God's Will for our Lives?

1. God's will for every person is that they be saved and follow Him.

2. God's will for us is that we love Him above all else, and that we love other people as we love ourselves.

3. God's will for us is that we trust Him.

4. God's will for us is that we are not anxious about our lives, but that we pray about everything.

5. God's will for us is that we become the persons that He uniquely made us to be – for His glory and purposes.

6. God's will is that whatever we do with our lives, it is all for His glory.

Study Questions

1. Thinking back to the start of our chapter where we looked at Mary's example to us, what do you think she meant when she said, 'I am a servant of the Lord.'?

2. How do you think Mary's view of herself as the Lord's servant made her able to accept God's will for her life, and even give Him thanks for it?

3. Do you see yourself as a servant of the Lord? If not, who are you a servant of?

▼ more...

How does who you serve influence the decisions you make in your life?

4. What do you think makes it so hard for us to always be willing to be used by God for His purposes?

   What do you think we need to do about it?

5. Think back to the six principles of making sure we are walking in God's will.

   1. To be saved

   2. Love God and love others

   3. Trust the Lord

   4. Don't be anxious

   5. Be who God made you to be

   6. Live your life for God's glory

   Which one(s) do you find hardest? Why? What can you do about it?

Let's Pray Together

Dear God, thank you for giving us principles that can guide us through life. Thank you that it is your will for all people to be saved. For any of our family and friends that don't love you – please will you save them. Thank you that we don't need to be anxious about our future because you are in control and we can trust you. Please help us to live by the principles in your Bible, which will make our paths straight and bring honour and glory to you. Amen.

TRUST IN THE LORD WITH ALL YOUR
HEART, AND DO NOT LEAN ON YOUR
OWN UNDERSTANDING. IN ALL YOUR
WAYS ACKNOWLEDGE HIM, AND HE
WILL MAKE STRAIGHT YOUR PATHS.
(PROVERBS 3:5-6)

MY ACTION PLAN

1.

2.

3.

4.

5.

What does the
Bible Say about...

Education?

Think

Ask

Bible

I wonder if you have ever thought about the reason for education? In fact, let's take it a step back. Let's think about what education is. Education is the way in which we gain knowledge. Most likely right now you are a student. You might attend a school, you might do correspondence school, or you might be home-educated. All of these ways are part of the process of gaining knowledge. But why is it so important that we be educated, anyway? And what should we be learning? What exactly does the Bible teach about education? Well, the Bible teaches us many principles about our learning.

Did You Know ...?

Some of the oldest school textbooks discovered are dated 2,500 years before the birth of Christ!

The Bible teaches us that ...

1. Knowledge begins with fearing God.

The fear of the Lord is the beginning of knowledge.

—Proverbs 1:7a

The book of Proverbs was mostly written by King Solomon. He was God's appointed king over Israel (you might remember his dad, King David). Solomon was known for his great wisdom, but how did he become so wise to begin with?

> At Gibeon the Lord appeared to Solomon in a dream by night, and God said, 'Ask what I shall give you.' And Solomon said, 'You have shown great and steadfast love to your servant David my father, because he walked before you in faithfulness, in righteousness, and

in uprightness of heart towards you. And you have kept for him this great and steadfast love and have given him a son to sit on his throne this day. And now, O LORD my God, you have made your servant king in place of David my father, although I am but a little child. I do not know how to go out or come in. And your servant is in the midst of your people whom you have chosen, a great people, too many to be numbered or counted for multitude. Give your servant therefore an understanding mind to govern your people, that I may discern between good and evil, for who is able to govern this your great people?' It pleased the Lord that Solomon had asked this. And God said to him, 'Because you have asked this, and have not asked for yourself long life or riches or the life of your enemies, but have asked for yourself understanding to discern what is right, behold, I now do according to your word. Behold, I give you a wise and discerning mind, so that none like you has been before you and none like you shall arise after you. I give you also what you have not asked, both riches and honour, so that no other king shall compare with you, all your days. And if you will walk in my ways, keeping my statutes and my commandments, as your father David walked, then I will lengthen your days."

—1 Kings 3:5-14

What is the first thing we notice about this passage? God appeared to Solomon in a dream to ask him what he would like. Wow! Why would God have appeared to Solomon and asked him such a question? Because Solomon, God's appointed man to lead Israel, loved God above all else.

Solomon loved the LORD, walking in the statutes of David his father.

—1 Kings 3:3a

God was with Solomon in this huge role of king, which came with enormous responsibility. But what God appointed Solomon to, He also prepared him for. He gave Solomon the great wisdom he needed.

When Solomon later wrote Proverbs, he wrote for us that the fear of the Lord was the beginning of knowledge. Did he mean that we had to be scared of God (like He was violent or vicious) in order to be able to learn things? No. To fear the Lord is to have a respectful awe of who God is and all He is capable of. And then we respond to God with that 'fear' in our minds.

Perhaps you have read the C.S. Lewis Narnia books. In *The Lion, the Witch and the Wardrobe*, where the girl, Susan, speaks with Mr. Beaver about Aslan the Lion (Aslan represents God):

'Aslan is a lion – the Lion, the great Lion.'

'Ooh' said Susan. 'I'd thought he was a man. Is he – quite safe? I shall feel rather nervous about meeting a lion.'

'Safe?' said Mr. Beaver … 'Who said anything about safe? 'Course he isn't safe. But he's good. He's the King, I tell you.'[1]

A right fear of God is the beginning of knowledge. Why? Because knowledge of who God is, is the most important information we will ever receive. Really? Yes, really. Your eternal life depends on it, and what can be more important than that? So, above all, make sure that you are a good student of God's Word, the Bible.

Let the word of Christ dwell in you richly, teaching and admonishing one another in all wisdom, singing psalms and hymns and spiritual songs, with thankfulness in your hearts to God.

—Colossians 3:16

---

1. C.S. Lewis, *The Lion, the Witch and the Wardrobe* (HarperTrophy), July 1994, page 86.

In order to allow God's Word to dwell richly in us, we need to be regularly reading it, memorising it, thinking about it and asking God to help us to apply it to our everyday lives. Are there some things here that you can be working on this week?

2. We are to Use God's Word as a Filter for our Education.

Therefore, as you received Christ Jesus the Lord, so walk in him, rooted and built up in him and established in the faith, just as you were taught, abounding in thanksgiving. See to it that no one takes you captive by philosophy and empty deceit, according to human tradition, according to the elemental spirits of the world, and not according to Christ.

—Colossians 2:6-8

The above verses are taken from a letter the apostle Paul wrote to the church in Colossae. It was a relatively new church, probably started by a man called Epaphras. Paul needed to write to the Colossian church because at the time there was a false teaching that had come into the church and it was gathering a following of people – sadly even people who said they were Christians. The false teaching was called 'gnosticism', and it's difficult for us to understand exactly what it was – but although people who followed it said they believed in Christ, they did not believe He was God's Son, nor did they believe that He was the way of salvation. That's a very dangerous teaching to follow, isn't it? Any teaching that does not teach Jesus Christ as the way of salvation is teaching a 'false gospel'. No wonder Paul needed to write to the Colossian church, to warn them of how dangerous this false teaching was!

As we read in the Scripture verses above, Paul warns the church about not being taken captive by philosophy and empty deceit, according to human tradition. He's basically saying, 'Don't follow man-made ideas and teachings if they are not in agreement with what the Bible teaches'. That makes sense, doesn't it? If God has perfect knowledge about us and this world that He created, it wouldn't make sense for us to believe someone who disagrees with God.

This is called 'using God's Word as a filter'. Do you know what a filter is? Its job is to keep rubbish out and let the good stuff pass through. Like a filter tap for our drinking water. The filter is a very fine piece of mesh that the water passes over. The mesh collects any little bits of rubbish that shouldn't be in the water and allows the pure, clean water to pass through. That's what the Bible should be to us. We should pass all the teaching we receive through God's Word – then all the 'rubbish' becomes easy to identify and get rid of. But of course, to be able to use God's Word as a filter, we must know it. Read it, study it, memorise it, pray it—and apply it!

3. We must Understand that the Ability to Learn comes only from God.

For you formed my inward parts; you knitted me together in my mother's womb. I praise you, for I am fearfully and wonderfully made. Wonderful are your works; my soul knows it very well.

—Psalm 139:13-14

Why is it so important for us to be reminded that our ability to learn comes from God? There are a couple of reasons for that. The first reason is that it is a great comfort to us.

There are times in our lives when it becomes glaringly obvious to us, and perhaps to others around us, that there are some things we are 'not good at'. Perhaps there has been a poor test score in maths, a bad mark on a project, or spelling words that just don't seem to come out right no matter how hard you try. Now, of course, if poor marks on a test are because we have not put in the effort to learn and study, or because of laziness or poor planning – well, this paragraph is not for you! But if you have tried your very best, and yet your best hasn't produced the result you hoped for, it's okay. It really is. The Lord God is sovereign (in control) over your brain agility! He has uniquely wired you in a certain way and while fractions might not be your thing right now, perhaps music, English, history, sewing, cooking, serving others selflessly or sharing Scripture with others, might be. Your value as a person does not depend on how smart or brainy you might appear to others. Your value is actually shown in Christ's great love for you. Don't forget, Christ loves you so much, He actually died to pay the penalty for the sins you have committed.

> *… but God shows his love for us in that while we were still sinners, Christ died for us.*
>
> —Romans 5:8

The second reason for believing our abilities come from God, is that it protects us from pride. Isn't that wonderful? Knowledge of God and how God has made us, both comforts us and protects us. But how does it protect us from pride?

> *For by the grace given to me I say to every one among you not to think of himself more highly than he ought to think, but to think with sober judgement, each according to the measure of faith God has assigned.*
>
> —Romans 12:3

> *When pride comes, then comes disgrace, but with the humble is wisdom.*
>
> —Proverbs 11:2

Pride is a terrible thing. The Bible tells us that all who are prideful will surely be humbled.

> *Therefore it says, 'God opposes the proud, but gives grace to the humble.'*
>
> —James 4:6b

4. We must Learn and be Educated to the Glory of God.

> *So, whether you eat or drink, or whatever you do, do all to the glory of God.*
>
> —1 Corinthians 10:31

I wonder if you are scratching your head about now, wondering what that means? Does it mean that you must go to Bible School to be able to learn to the glory of God? No, not at all.

Whatever you do, do it for God's glory. That means that even in our studying and education we are to seek God's glory. How do we do that? We are to make sure that our attitudes towards our schooling and learning bring honour to God. We also need to make sure that our behaviour towards those who teach us and those who we learn with is Christ-like. We also need to make sure that the things we are learning are honouring to God and His Word. And finally, regardless of how much we may like or dislike what we have to learn, we are to give God glory by doing our best in it.

5. We need to Make sure our Reason for our Education is Honouring to God.

Ultimately, the reason we are educated is so that we can one day do something with that learning. It might be to pursue a career or to use that knowledge or skill to serve others. You might already be thinking about this already, and no doubt you've heard the question that adults love to ask, 'What do you want to be when you grow up?' Whatever the answer might be, make sure your desires behind it are right.

Be careful of choosing a certain education because you want to earn the most money you can. The Bible warns us that we cannot serve the god of money and the God of the Bible.

> *No one can serve two masters, for either he will hate the one and love the other, or he will be devoted to the one and despise the other. You cannot serve both God and money.*
>
> —Matthew 6:24

> *Whatever you do, work heartily, as for the Lord and not for men, knowing that from the Lord you will receive the inheritance as your reward. You are serving the Lord Christ.*
>
> —Colossians 3:23-24

This verse reminds us not to look for the praise and compliments of others as we study, learn and work. Work at your education heartily (with your whole heart) for the Lord.

But wait, there's more!

What other Principles can we Learn from Scripture?

Bible

There was once a young man who had many things. The things that he owned showed that he was very wealthy, and his things were very important to him. But there was one thing that he did not have, and he did not know how he could get it. His money could not buy it for him – otherwise he would have had it already. So he went to the right person to ask where he could get this precious thing from.

And behold, a man came up to him [Jesus], saying, 'Teacher, what good deed must I do to have eternal life?' And he said to him, 'Why do you ask me about what is good? There is only one who is good. If you would enter life, keep the commandments.' He said to him, 'Which ones?' And Jesus said, 'You shall not murder, You shall not commit adultery, You shall not steal, You shall not bear false witness, Honour your father and mother, and, You shall love your neighbour as yourself.' The young man said to him, 'All these I have kept. What do I still lack?' Jesus said to him, 'If you would be perfect, go, sell what you possess and give to the poor, and you will have treasure in heaven; and come, follow me.' When the young man heard this he went away sorrowful, for he had great possessions.

—Matthew 19:16-22

The young man wanted to know how he could be saved and he went straight to the right person to ask. But what Jesus said might seem

▼ *more...*

strange. He told the young man to sell all his possessions. Is that the way to receive eternal life? No, because we know that in order to be saved, we must believe in Jesus, turn from our sin and follow Him. So why did He tell the young man to sell his precious things? Jesus knew that the young man did not value eternal life enough. He wanted to teach the young man that his possessions were too important to him—so important, that he would rather have his things than eternal life. Things are temporary, they don't last forever. Our lives do. But the young man made his decision. He went away without eternal life with Jesus – and without understanding that his possessions were more important to him than his soul.

The young man went in pursuit of the most important information that we could ever have. And the sad thing is that he went away without the very thing he was looking for. He rejected the education that Jesus was offering him. To learn how we can truly be saved is the most important education we can ever receive. Do you know how a person can be saved from the penalty for their sin?

What did we Learn about Education?

Ask

1. Knowledge begins with fearing God.

2. We are to use God's Word to filter our education.

3. The ability to learn comes from God.

4. We must learn and be educated to the glory of God.

5. We are to work hard at our education.

6. The most important thing we can ever learn is what we must do to be saved.

Study Questions

The fear of the LORD is the beginning of knowledge.
—Proverbs 1:7a

1. What attitudes or behaviours do you think show that we 'fear God' in the right way?

2. Fearing God helps us to have a right view of ourselves. It reminds us that we are created by God, and that helps us to be humble and ready to submit to His Word.

   Why do you think that fearing God is the best way for us to begin building our knowledge about life and the world around us?

3. God created knowledge and it is a privilege to receive an education. What things in your education are you thankful for?

4. What principles did you learn in this chapter that have helped you?

5. What principles in this chapter do you think you need to put into practice?

Let's Pray Together

Dear God, thank you for what we have learnt about education from your Word, the Bible. Thank you for telling us that fearing you is the beginning of knowledge. Please help us to fear you in a right way – a way that reminds us of how great you are, and how awesome your works are. Thank you for the way in which you created us, with the ability to learn. And thank you for all that we have learnt. May knowing the way of salvation be the thing we hold most dear. Please help us to learn well, to work hard and to honour you in all that we study and do. Amen.

THEREFORE, AS YOU RECEIVED CHRIST JESUS AS LORD, SO WALK IN HIM, ROOTED AND BUILT UP IN HIM AND ESTABLISHED IN THE FAITH, JUST AS YOU WERE TAUGHT, ABOUNDING IN THANKSGIVING. SEE TO IT THAT NO ONE TAKES YOU CAPTIVE BY PHILOSOPHY AND EMPTY DECEIT, ACCORDING TO HUMAN TRADITION, ACCORDING TO THE ELEMENTAL SPIRITS OF THE WORLD, AND NOT ACCORDING TO CHRIST. (COLOSSIANS 2:6-8)

MY ACTION PLAN

1.

2.

3.

4.

5.

Look out for the next book in THINK. ASK. BIBLE.

GOD'S WORD AND YOU
by Laura Martin

You've got a mind – use it! If you've got questions – ask them! But don't fill your mind with rubbish and it is important to ask the right questions. So how do you make sure that you're headed in the right direction? Well – THINK, ASK – BIBLE! God's Word is the crucial ingredient. Read it – study it – learn it – think about it. God's Word will help you with your questions about family, friends and other important stuff like work and worry, troubles and trials and even your body. Find out about how David, Jonathan, Joseph, Martha and others experienced the same issues you do every day of your life – and how God is the same all powerful God for you as He was for them.

Extra Features: Study Questions and Prayers
ISBN: 978-1-78191-821-0

CHRISTIAN FOCUS PUBLICATIONS

Christian Focus   Christian Heritage   CF4K   Mentor

Christian Focus Publications publishes books for adults and children under its four main imprints: Christian Focus, CF4K, Mentor and Christian Heritage. Our books reflect our conviction that God's Word is reliable and Jesus is the way to know him, and live for ever with him.

Our children's publication list includes a Sunday school curriculum that covers pre-school to early teens, and puzzle and activity books. We also publish personal and family devotional titles, biographies and inspirational stories that children will love.

If you are looking for quality Bible teaching for children then we have an excellent range of Bible stories and age-specific theological books.

From pre-school board books to teenage apologetics, we have it covered!

Find us at our web page:
www.christianfocus.com

CF4 •K
Because you're never
too young to know Jesus